The Bumblebees

by: Linda Edwards

AuthorHouse™ LLC
1663 Liberty Drive
Bloomington, IN 47403
www.authorhouse.com
Phone: 1-800-839-8640

© 2013 Linda Edwards. All Rights Reserved.

No part of this book may be reproduced, stored in a retrieval system, or transmitted by any means without the written permission of the author.

Published by AuthorHouse 10/04/2013

ISBN: 978-1-4817-5939-7 (sc)
978-1-4817-5940-3 (e)

Library of Congress Control Number: 2013911100

Any people depicted in stock imagery provided by Thinkstock are models, and such images are being used for illustrative purposes only.
Certain stock imagery © Thinkstock.

This book is printed on acid-free paper.

Because of the dynamic nature of the Internet, any web addresses or links contained in this book may have changed since publication and may no longer be valid. The views expressed in this work are solely those of the author and do not necessarily reflect the views of the publisher, and the publisher hereby disclaims any responsibility for them.

authorHOUSE®

The Bumblebees

Where do the bumblebees go?
When it rains
Where do the bumblebees go?

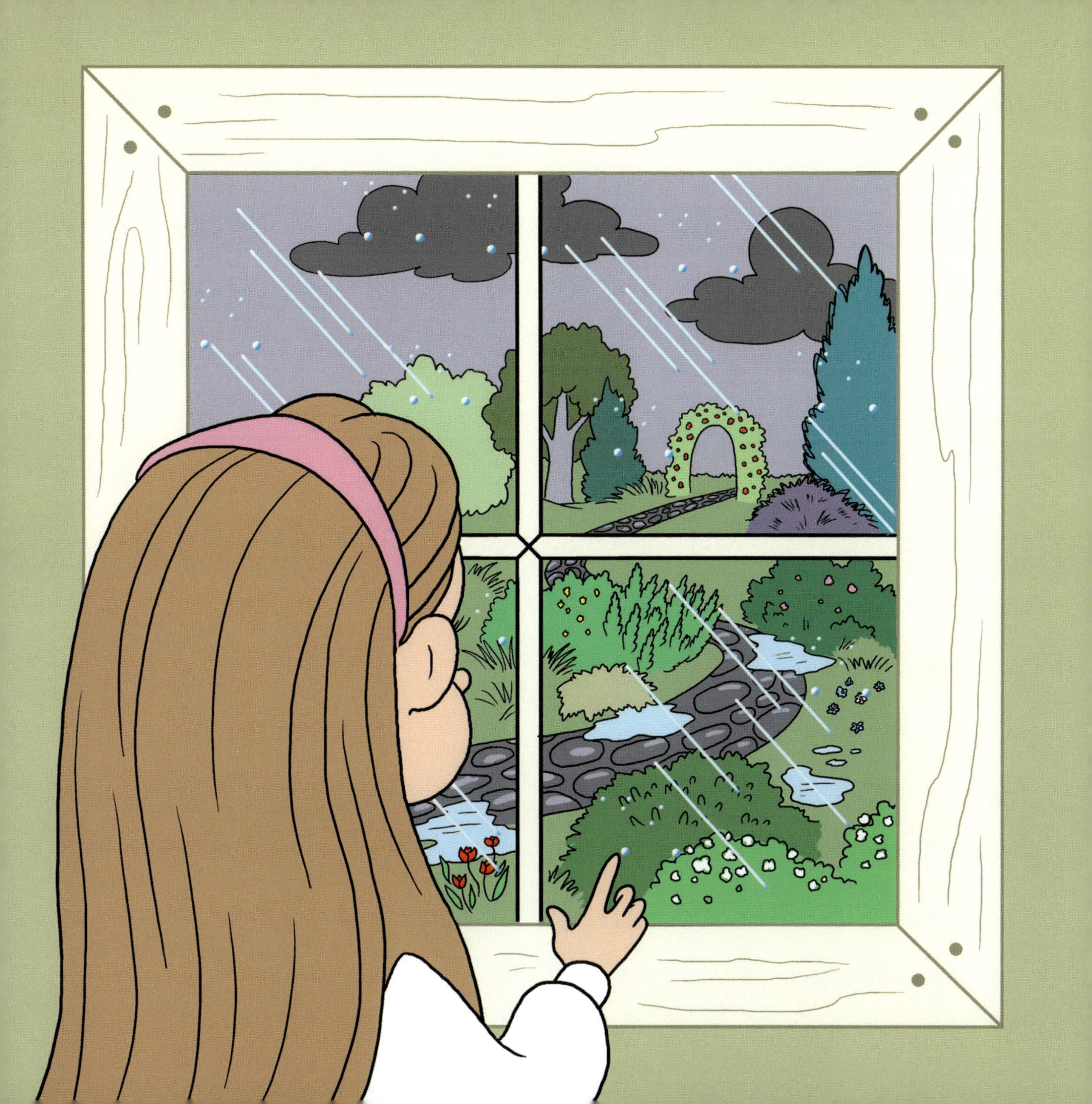

Do they run for cover
Beneath giant blades of grass
To a secret hiding place?

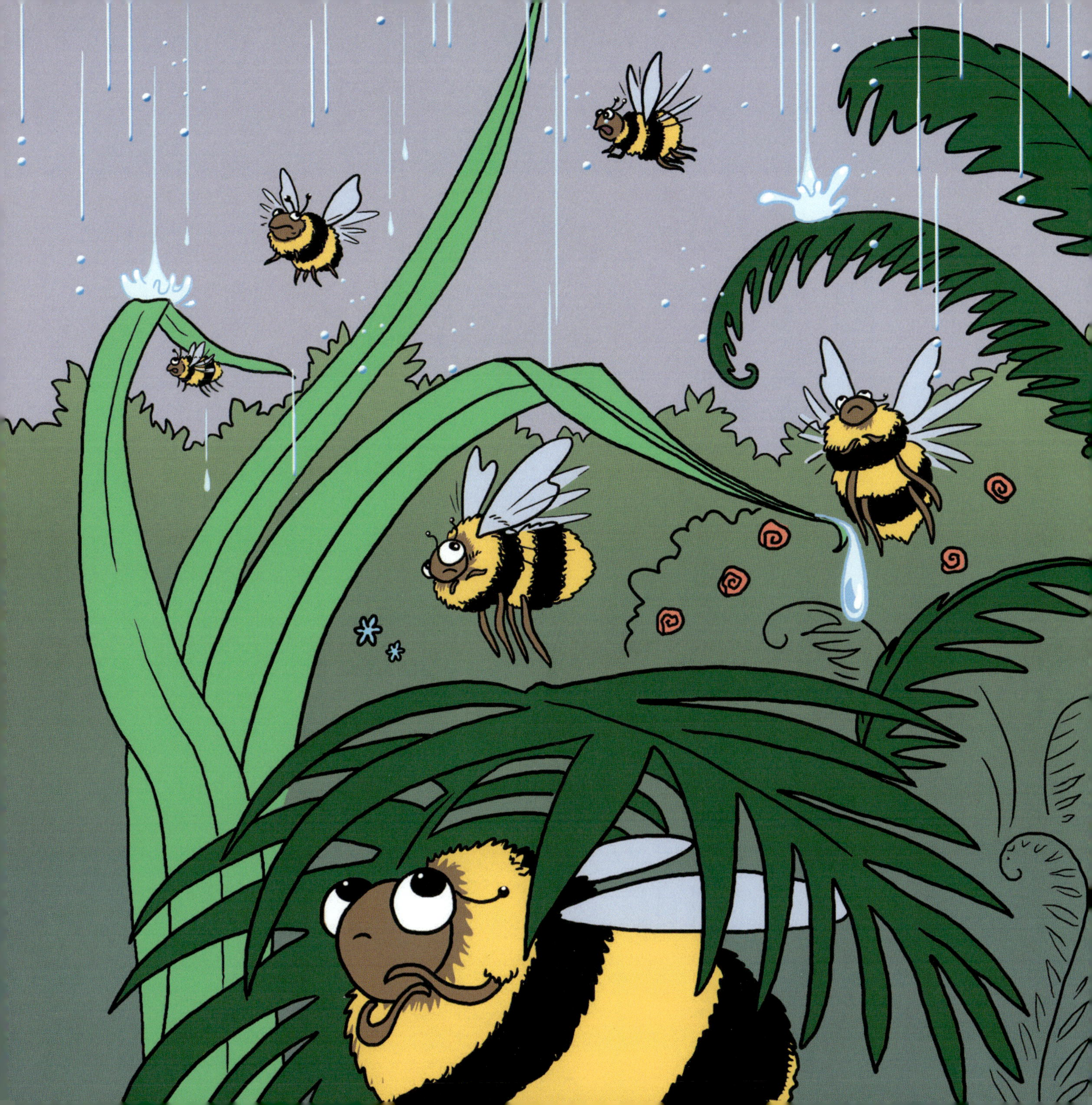

Do they open bumblebee umbrellas
On a rainy day
Or put on yellow slickers, to
Keep the rain away.

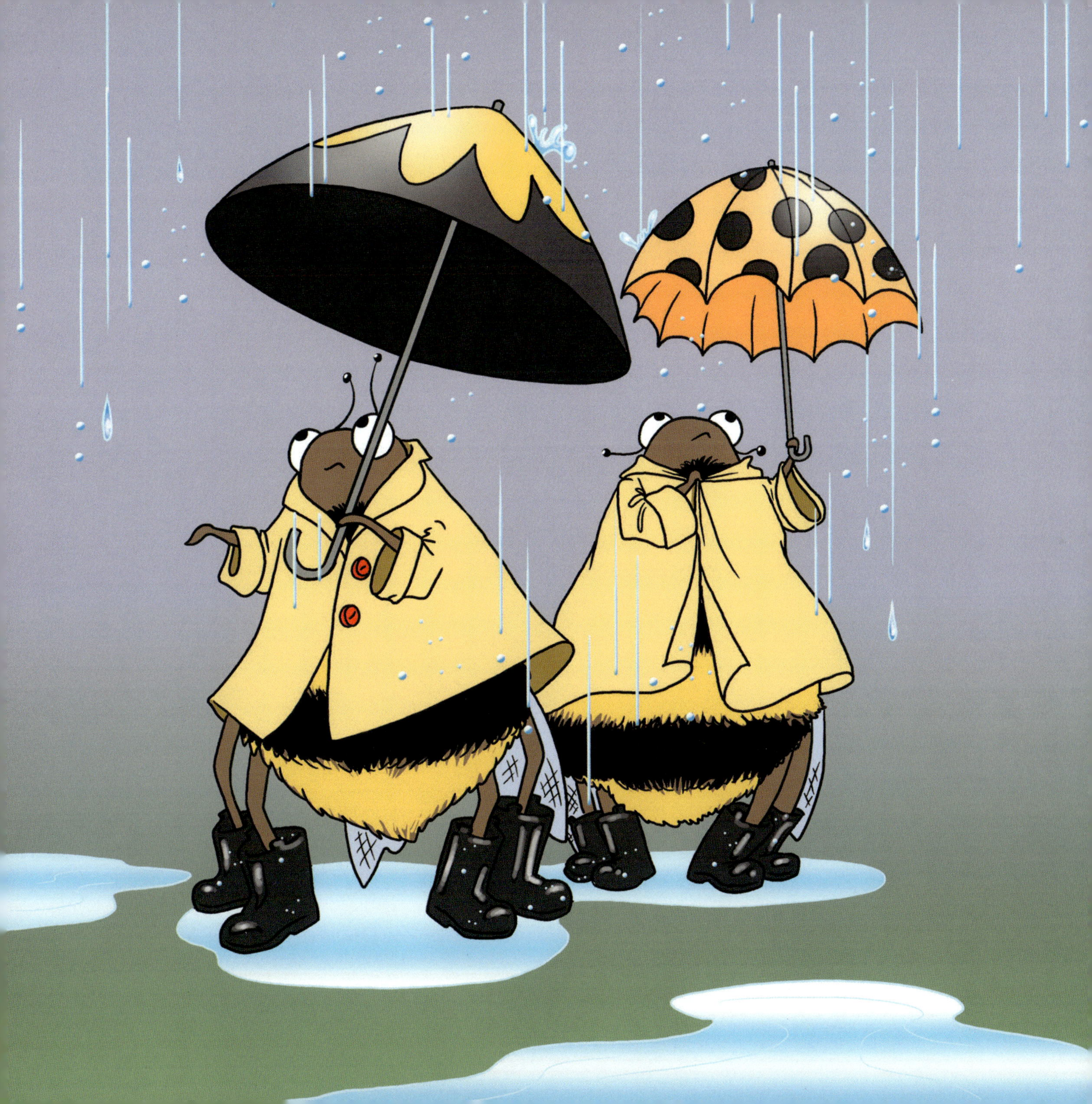

OH WHERE DO THE BUMBLEBEES GO?

Where do the bumblebees fly,

when it pours

Is it to their tiny houses, behind,

Black and yellow doors?

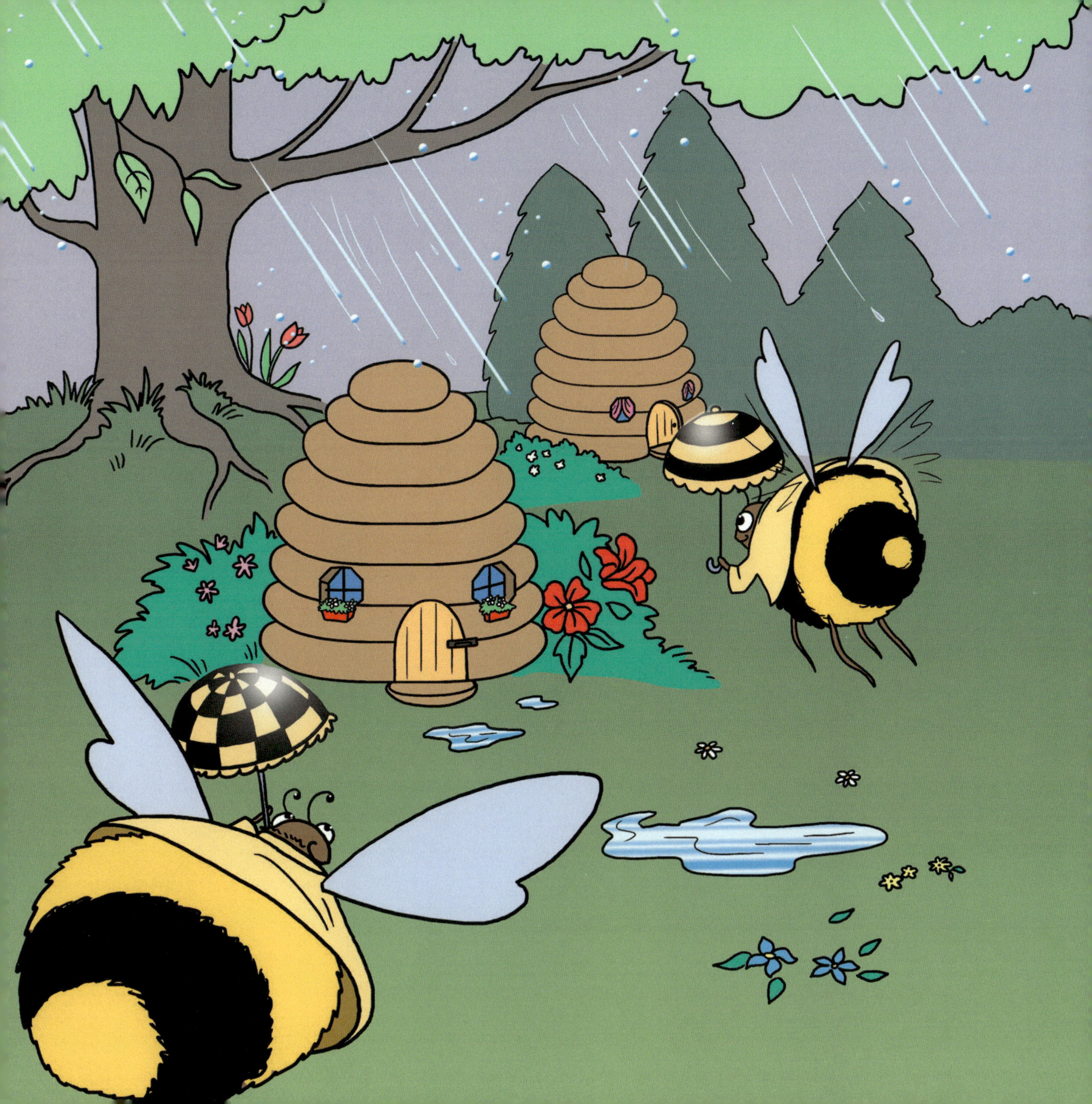

OH WHERE DO THE BUMBLEBEES GO?

On the darkest and rainiest night

When the flowers close
up for the day

Oh, where do the bumblebees stay?

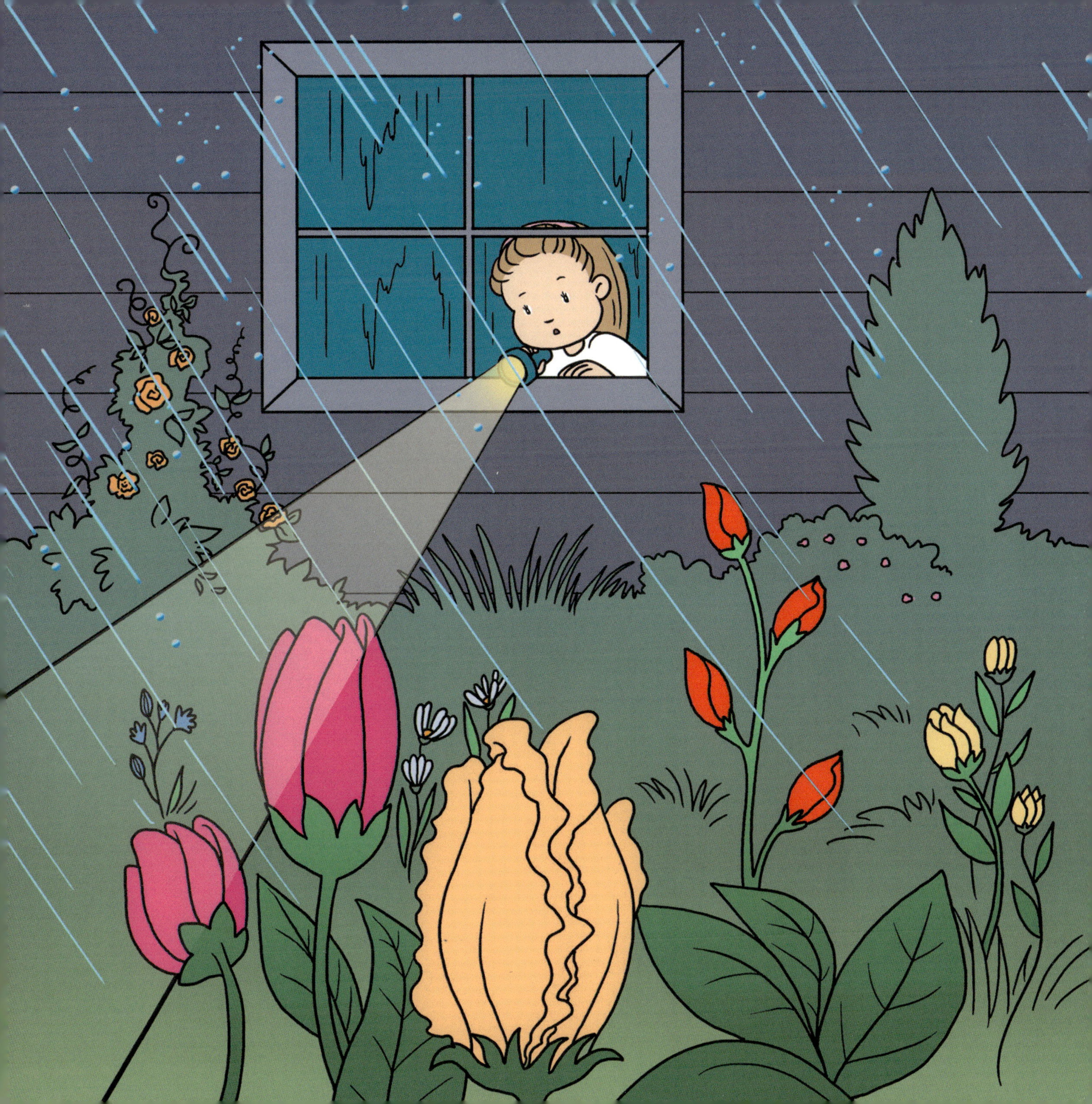

Do the bumblebees sleep in
Tiny brass beds when it rains?
Watching the rain drops fall,
Off their pollen covered
window panes?

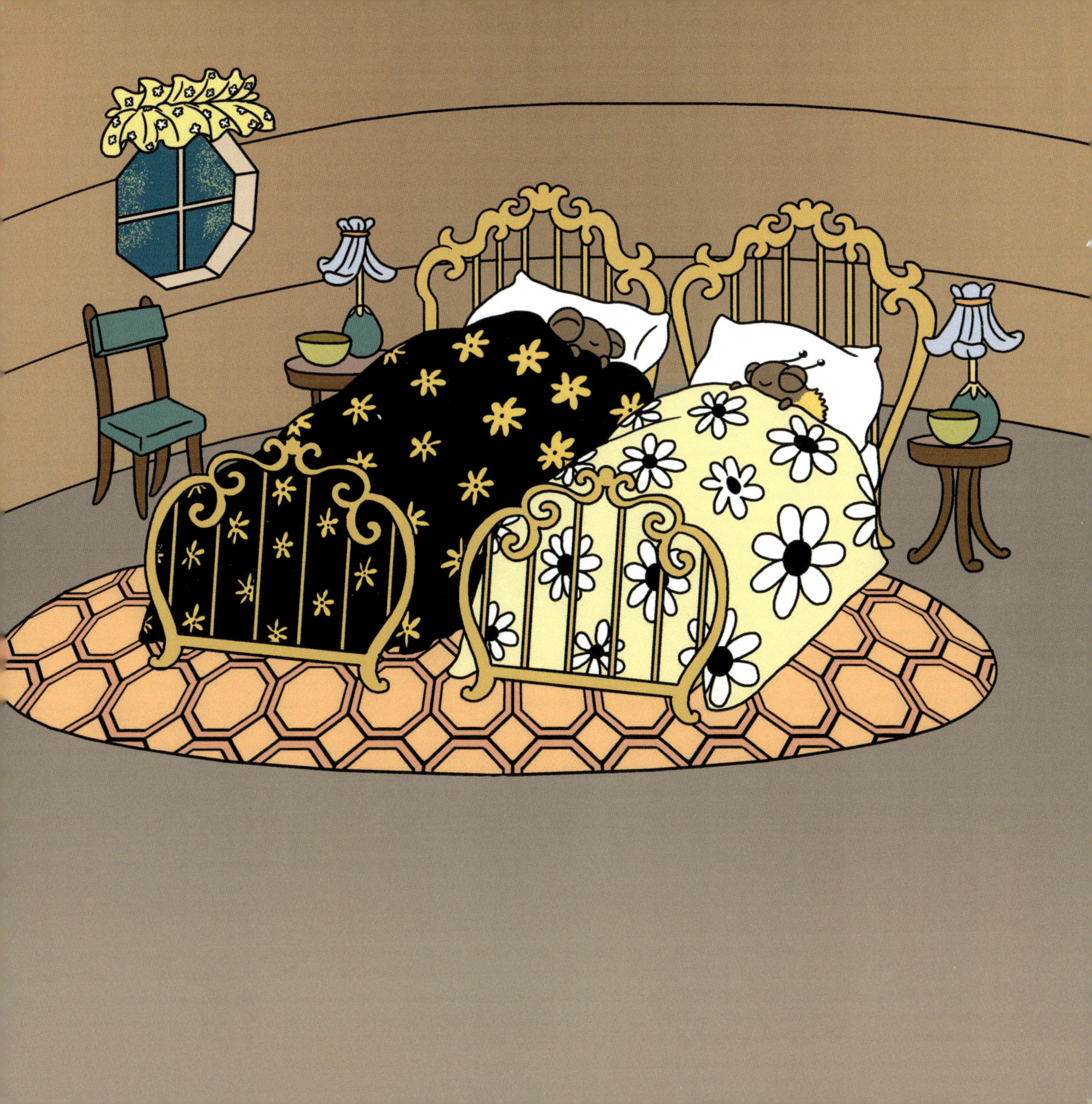

Or do they read scary tales,
In their striped bumblebee pajamas
While stormy skies prevail,

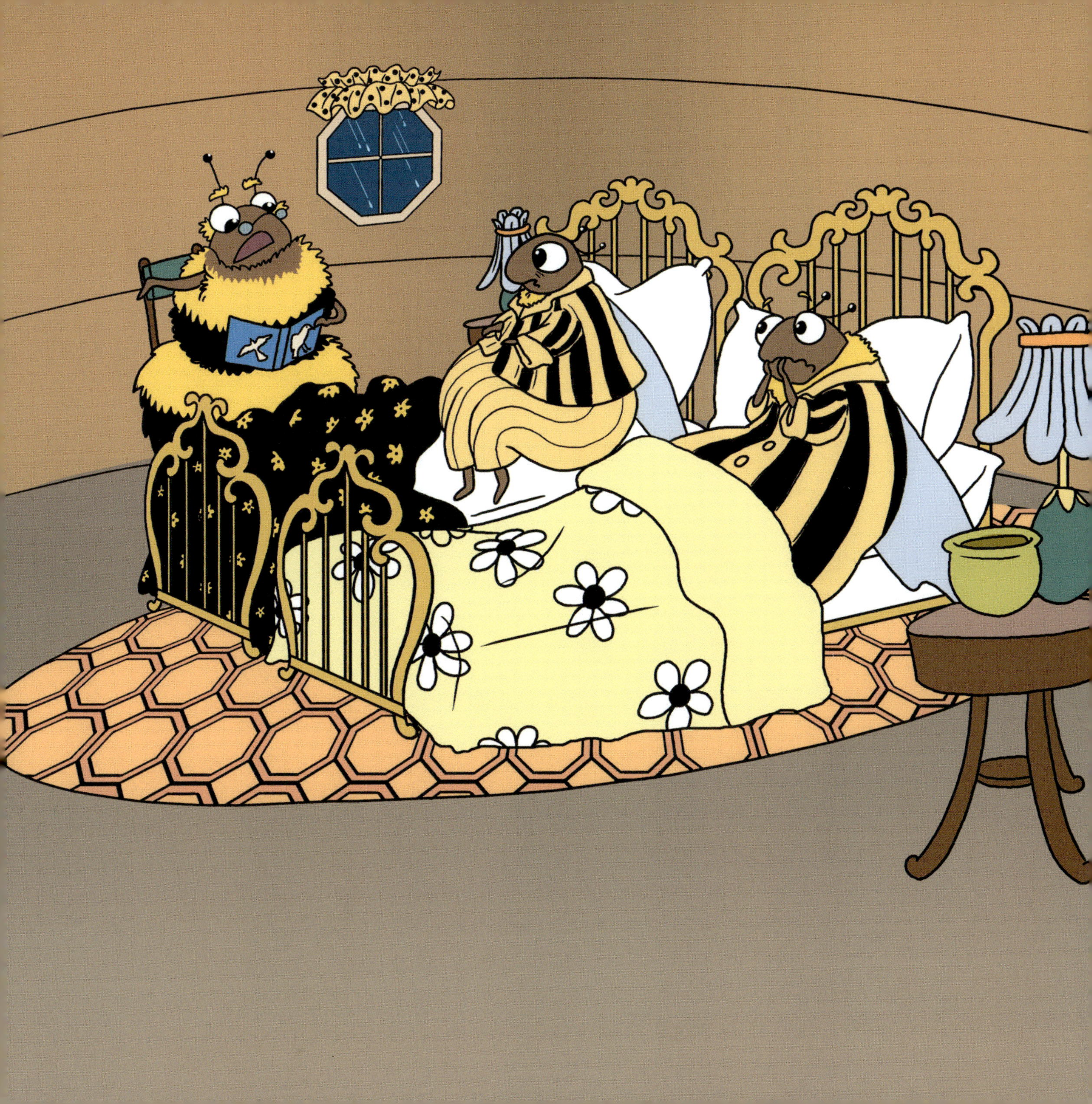

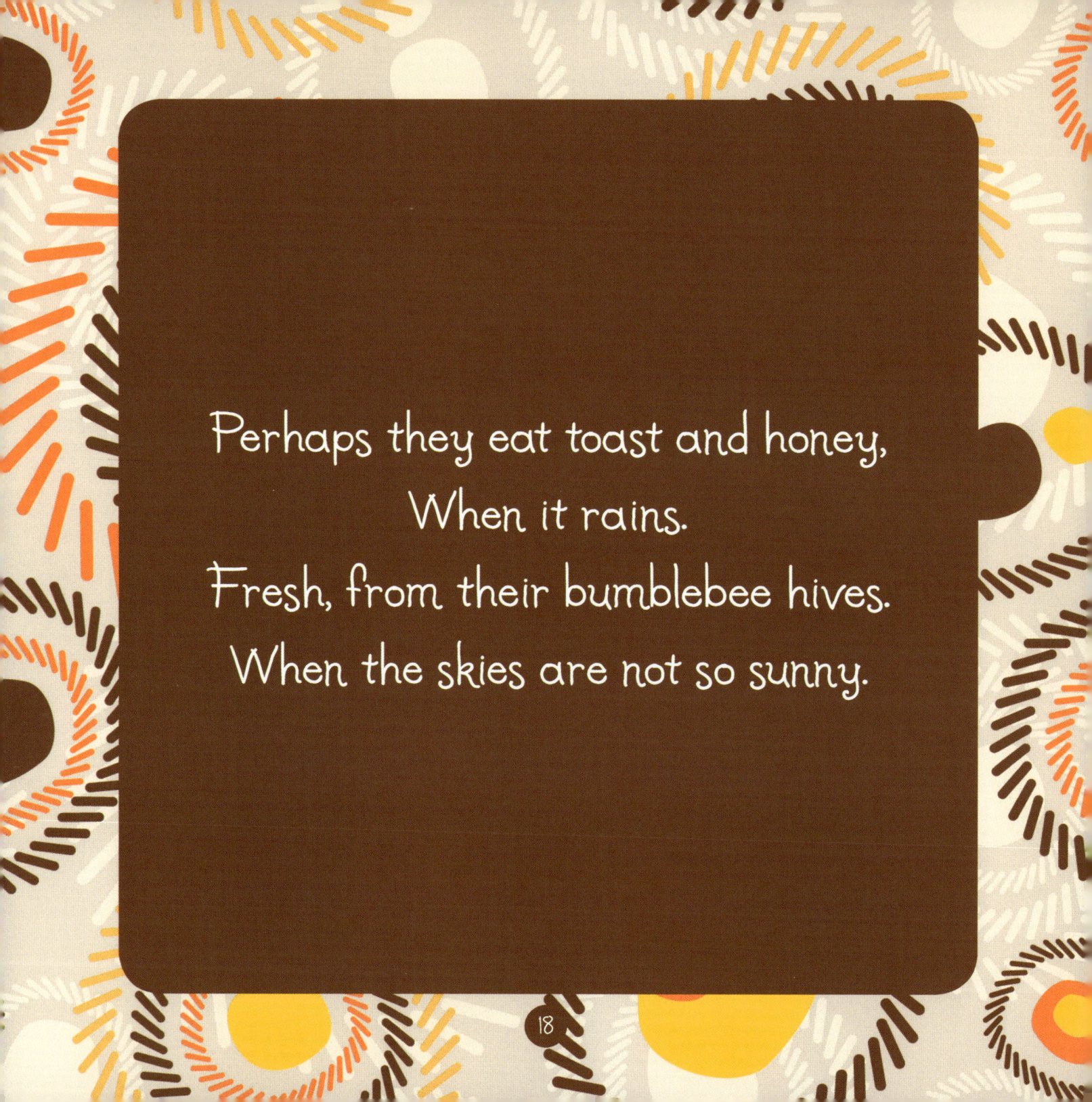

Perhaps they eat toast and honey,
When it rains.
Fresh, from their bumblebee hives.
When the skies are not so sunny.

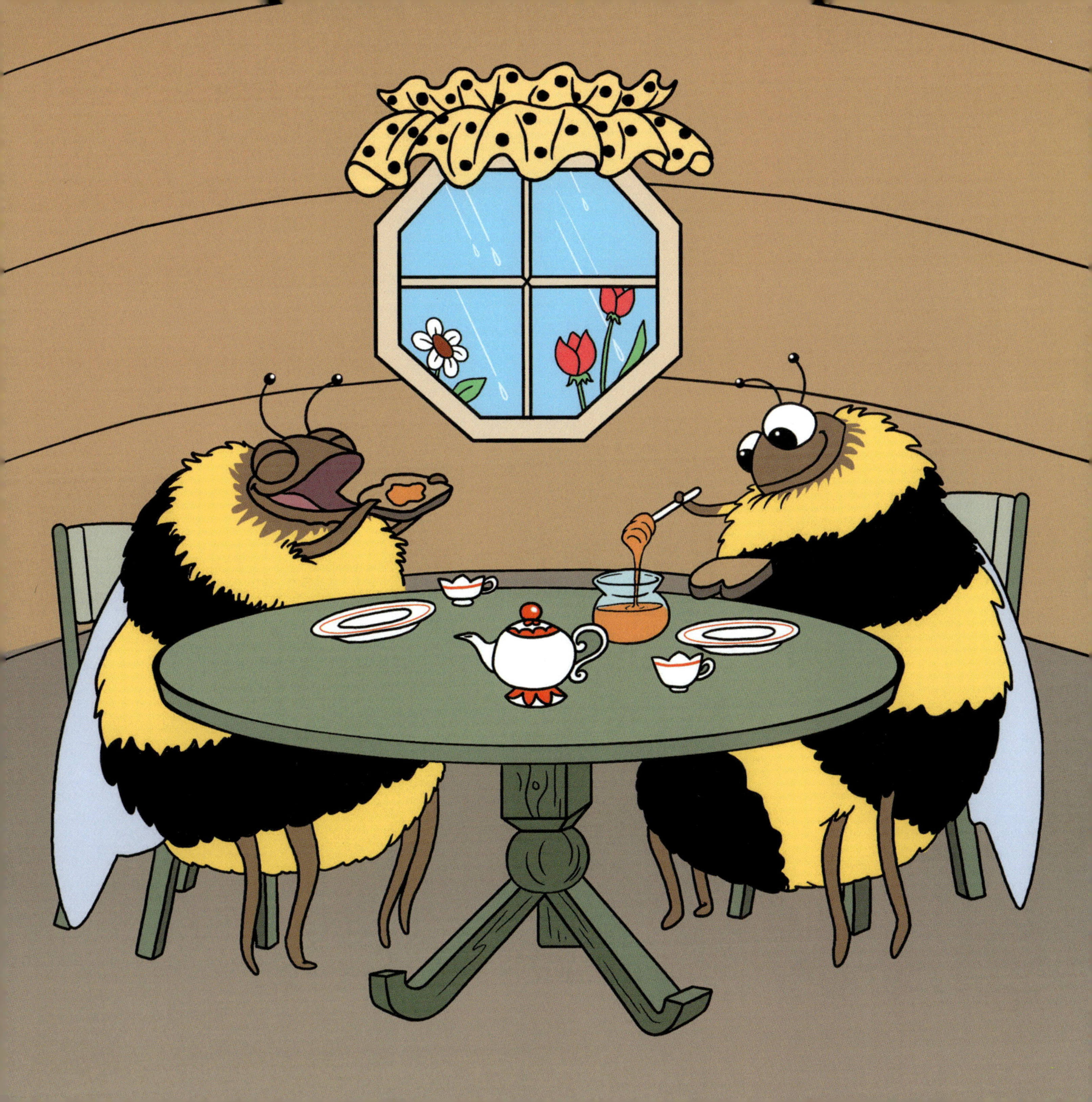

OH WHERE DO THE BUMBLEBEES GO WHEN IT RAINS?

OH WHERE DO THE BUMBLEBEES GO?

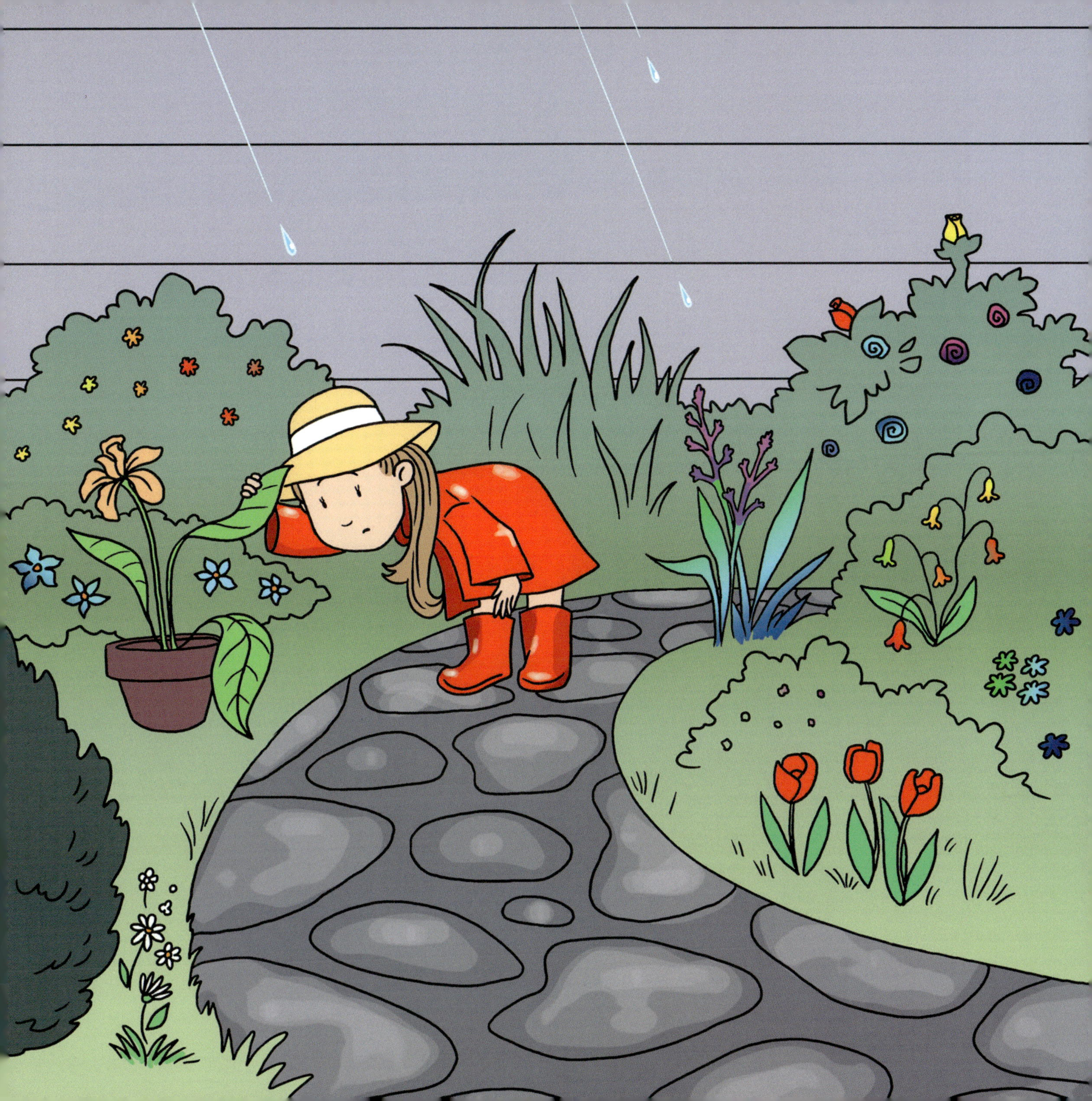

Well, where do you suppose?

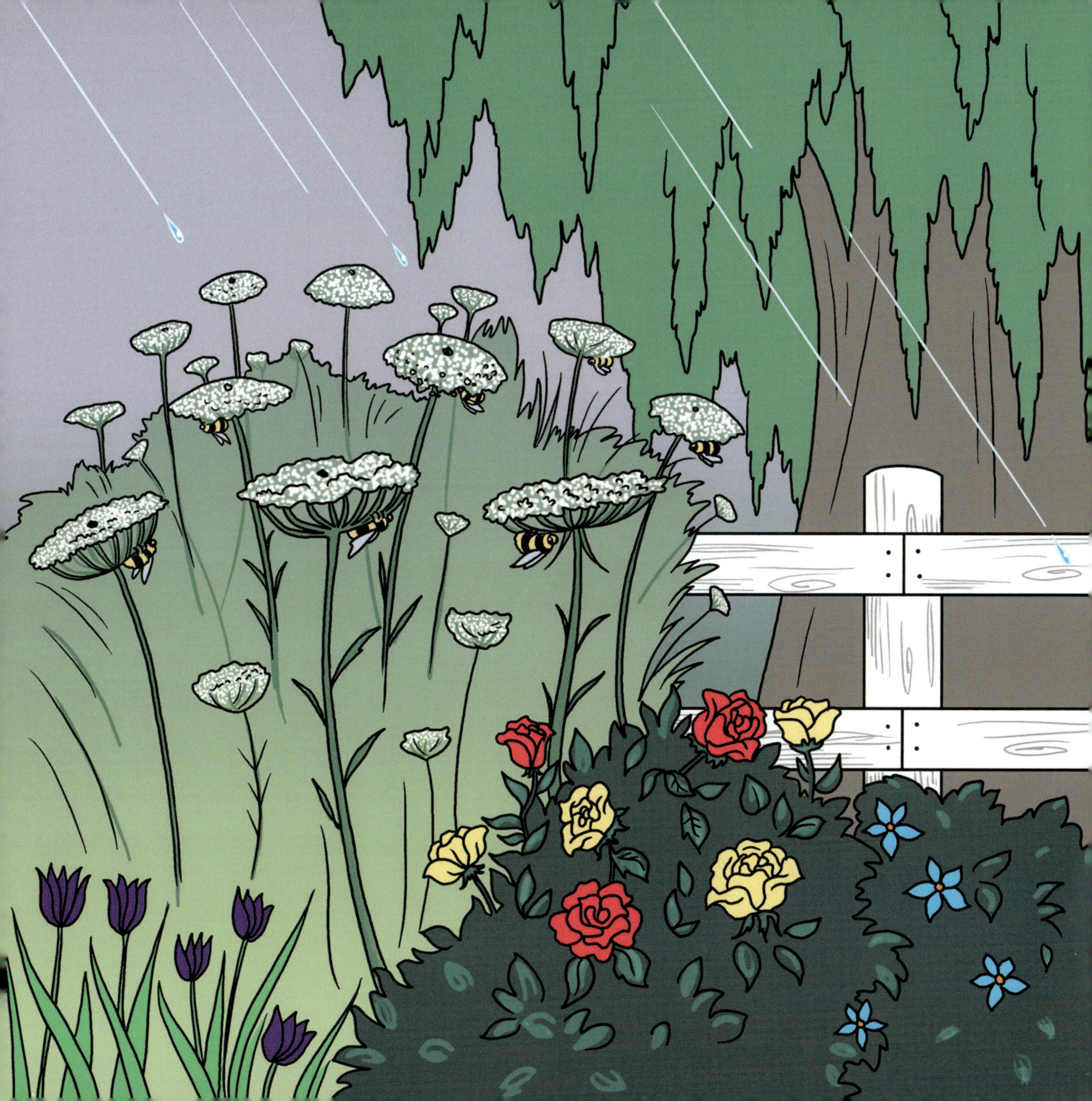

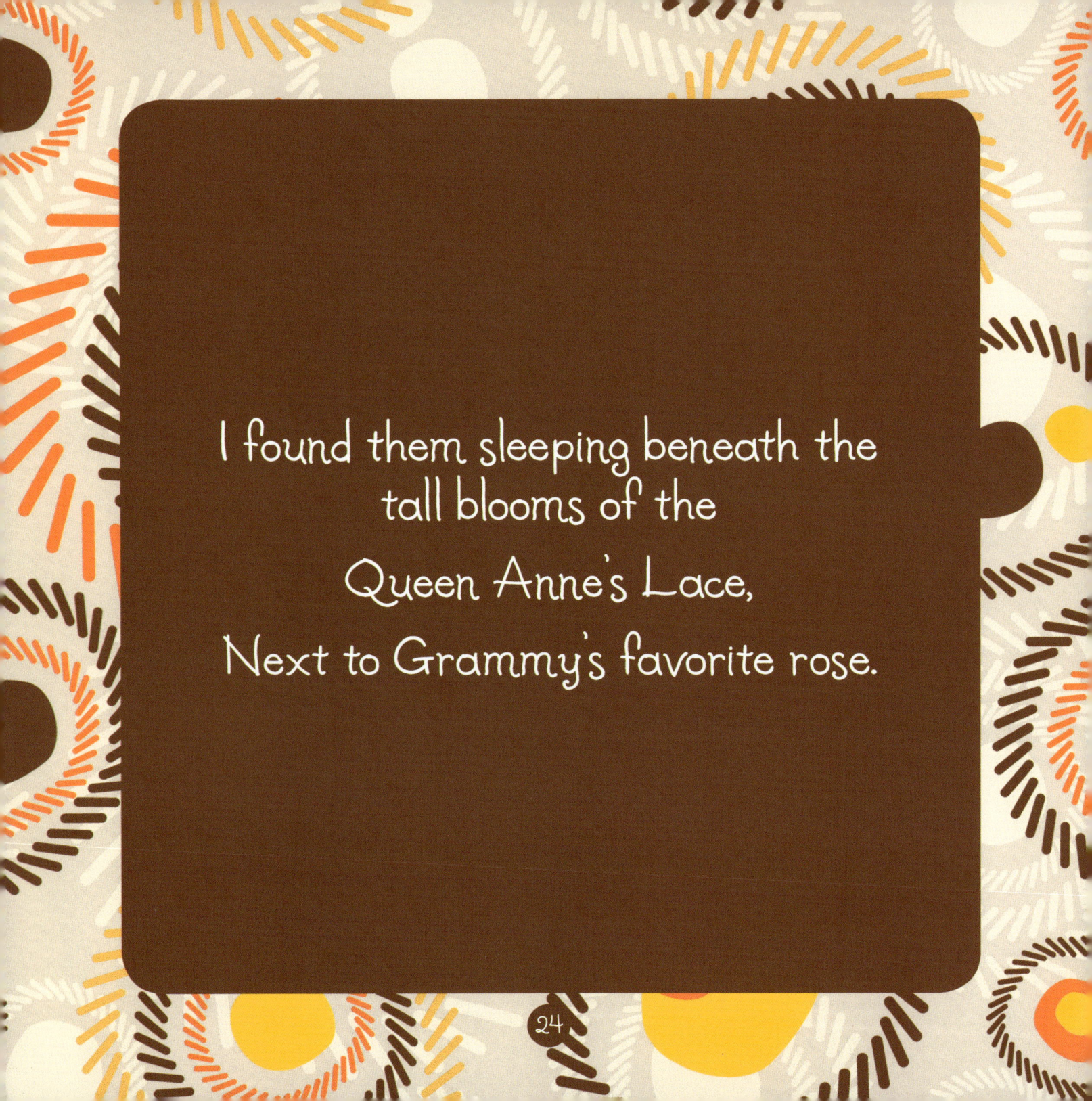

I found them sleeping beneath the
tall blooms of the
Queen Anne's Lace,
Next to Grammy's favorite rose.

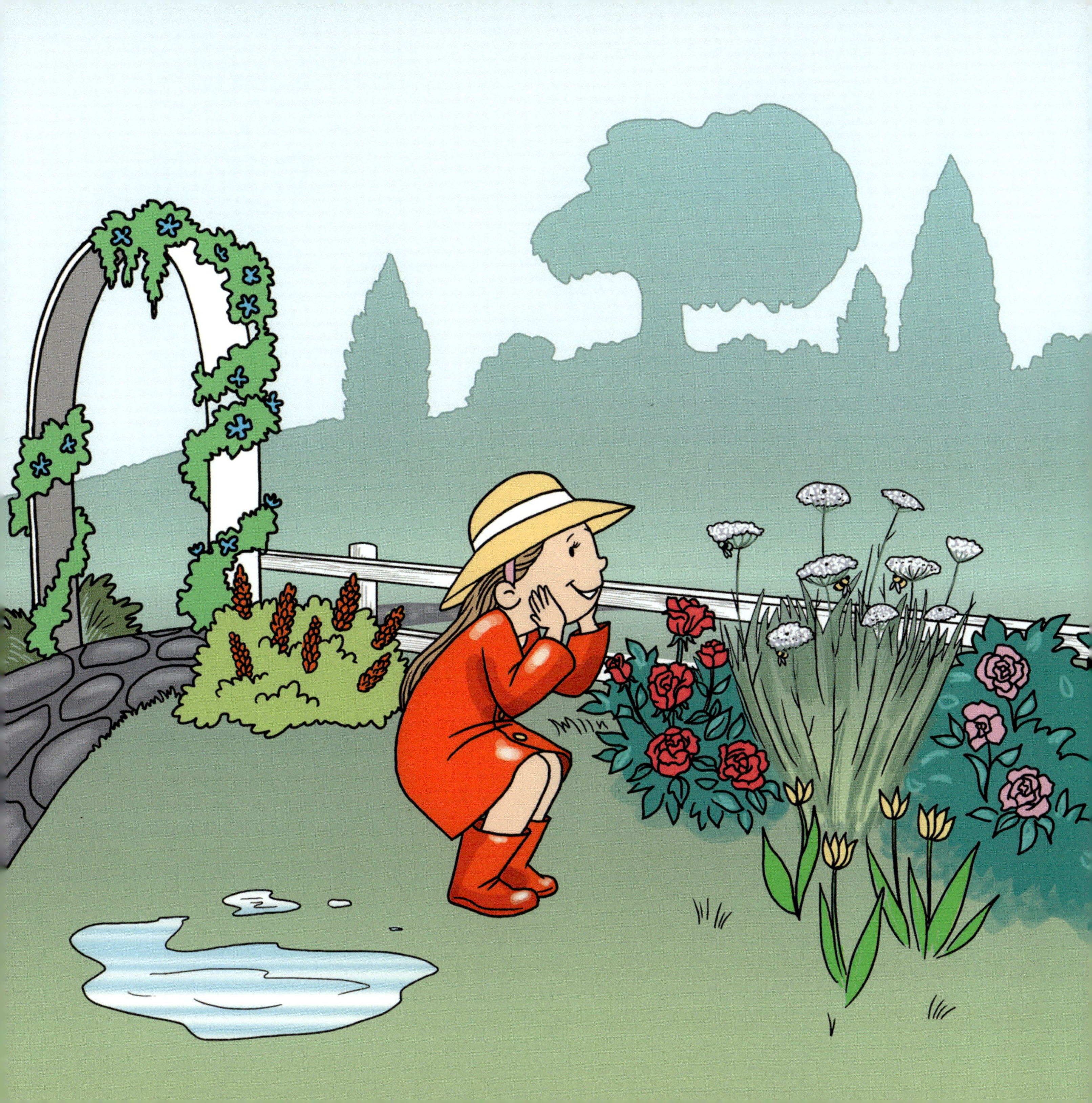

The End

CPSIA information can be obtained
at www.ICGtesting.com
Printed in the USA
LVIC060516310320
651738LV00001B/3